Your Book of Camping

The *Your Book* Series

Abbeys · Acting · Aeromodelling · Anglo-Saxon England · Animal Drawing · Aquaria · Archaeology · Astronomy · Ballet · Brasses · Breadmaking · Bridges · Butterflies and Moths · Camping · Canals · The Way a Car Works · Card Games · Chess · Contract Bridge · Corn Dollies · Mediaeval and Tudor Costume · Nineteenth Century Costume · Cricket · Dinghy Sailing · Embroidery · English Country Dancing · Fencing · Film-making · Fishes · Flower Arranging · Flower Making · Forestry · The Guitar · Gymnastics · Hovercraft · Judo · Kites · Knitted Toys · Knots · Landscape Drawing · Light · Magic · Men in Space · Mental Magic · Modelling · Money · Music · Painting · Paper Folding · Parliament · Party Games · Patchwork · Pet Keeping · Photography · Photographing Wild Life · Keeping Ponies · Prehistoric Animals · Prehistoric Britain · Pressed and Dried Flowers · Puppetry · Racing and Sports Cars · The Recorder · Roman Britain · Sea Fishing · The Seashore · Secret Writing · Self-Defence · Shell Collecting · Skating · Soccer · Space Travel · Swimming · Survival Swimming and Life Saving · Table Tennis · Table Tricks · Tall Ships · Television · Tennis · Traction Engines · Watching Wild Life · The Weather · Woodwork

YOUR BOOK OF **CAMPING**

D. T. Roscoe

FABER AND FABER
London · Boston

*First published in 1980
by Faber and Faber Limited
3 Queen Square London WC1N 3AU
Set, printed and bound in Great Britain by
Fakenham Press Limited, Fakenham, Norfolk*

All rights reserved
© *D. T. Roscoe 1980*

British Library Cataloguing in Publication Data

Roscoe, Donald Thomas
  Your book of camping. – (Your book series).
  1. Camping – Juvenile literature
  I. Title
  796.54   GV191.7

  ISBN 0–571–11521–7

FOR MARTIN AND BRIAN

Contents

1	Let's Go Camping	13
2	Choosing Your Tent	16
3	Pitching and Striking	26
4	Other Equipment	35
5	Packing Your Rucksack	45
6	Choosing a Campsite	48
7	Living in Your Tent	51
8	Bivouacs and Shelters	61
9	Cycle Camping and Canoe Camping	66
10	Looking After Your Camping Equipment	77
11	Camping Checklists and the Country Code	83
	Some More Books To Read	86

Illustrations

1	Ridge tent	18
2	Ridge tent with flysheet	19
3	Single pole and 'A' Pole	20
4	Tent supported by outside 'A' pole	20
5	Separator	21
6	Ridge pole	21
7	Pyramid tent	21
8	Ridge tent with bell end	22
9	Mountain tent with sleeve entrance	22
10	Wedge tent	22
11	Extended flysheet fitted to pyramid tent	23
12	Sleeve entrance	23
13	Effect of high side walls	23
14	Slider	24
15	Skewer and Bulldog tent pegs	24
16	Pole sections connected by cord	26
17	Tent erection 1	27
18	Tent erection 2	28
19	Tent erection 3	29
20	Tent erection 4	30
21	Tent erection 5	30
22	Tent erection 6	31
23	Correctly placed peg	31
24	Improving a poorly placed peg	31
25	Double pegging	32
26	Tent striking 1	33

Illustrations

27	Tent striking 2	*34*
28	Tent striking 3	*34*
29	Common types of camping stove	*37*
30	Improvised candle-holder	*41*
31	Tents are very inflammable!	*42*
32	A packframe with fitted sack in use in the Cairngorm Mountains, Scotland	*43*
33	Load carrying	*46*
34	A well-packed rucksack	*47*
35	Shelter	*49*
36	Avoid hollows!	*49*
37	Toaster	*53*
38	Canvas windshield	*56*
39	Drainage channel	*57*
40	Bivouac under an overhang	*62*
41	Bivouac sheet	*64*
42	Simple tent shelter	*64*
43	Wedge tent shelter	*65*
44	Awning	*65*
45	Cave adapted to make a shelter	*65*
46	Ian Hibell, cycle tourist extraordinary	*67*
47	Eskimo hunter in his kayak	*71*
48	Canadian canoe	*72*
49	Making a waterproof fastening on a canoe bag	*73*
50	Section through a one-pint paraffin stove	*79*
51	Nipple key in use	*80*

Acknowledgements

I would like to thank Doug Godlington for his cartoons, without which this book would not be quite the same, and for illustrations 9, 12, 30, 40 and 45; Ian Hibell for permission to print the photograph on page 167 (illustration 46); Doug Madge (Creative Photographers) for his work in preparing the photographs; John Webster for technical advice on my own drawings; and last but not least my wife, Barbara, for her help, advice and encouragement during all stages of preparation of the manuscript.

CHAPTER ONE

Let's Go Camping

Camping and shelter-making are as old as man himself. Throughout the history of man people have camped, not for pleasure but as a way of life. Armies have always camped during campaigns and wandering herdsmen and traders used to spend all their lives living in tents. The North American Indians and the Lapps of Northern Scandinavia both lived in wigwams, which were ideally suited to their wandering existence, following their herds or the animals which they hunted. Even today wandering, or 'nomadic', tribesmen still live in tents in the traditional way in many countries. The Tuaregs of the desert, the Kurdish herdsmen and many Lapps are still constantly on the move and their homes must move too. Even in Britain Gipsies and Tinkers camping in their 'howffs', rounded tents of canvas thrown over willow poles, were still a common sight less than fifty years ago. Camping for pleasure, however, is a comparatively new idea; it is great fun and can be exciting and adventurous too.

When we use the term camping it can mean one of two quite different things, 'standing' camps or 'lightweight' camps. You may have attended or seen a scout or guide camp at some time. This is what is meant by a standing camp. The tents are large and heavy, designed to sleep six or eight people, and you would find it very difficult indeed to carry such a tent any distance. This is why the camp is known as a standing camp; it is intended to stand in one spot and is usually situated very close to a road or track, as the heavy equipment has to be transported to the spot in a motor vehicle.

In this book we are concerned with lightweight camping. As the name implies, the equipment is comparatively light and compact, and the whole of your equipment and food can be carried in a rucksack. This type of camping offers a great deal of freedom. You are not dependent upon a particular form of transport. You can travel by car, bus or train to your starting point and from there you can walk right out into wild and remote country far from roads and habitation. You can even, as we shall see, pack your equipment on a bicycle and go straight from home to anywhere you please, or travel by canoe on the network of inland waterways which covers the whole of the country.

Lightweight camping can itself be sub-divided into two parts: 'mobile' and 'static' camping. Walking (or backpacking as it is coming to be known), cycling and canoeing are all aspects of mobile camping. Each day the mobile camper breaks camp and moves on to somewhere new, carrying his equipment with him. However, people camp for many different reasons. Some just like to be out of doors, camping for camping's sake. Many more camp to be as close as possible to mountains, cliffs, caves, rivers or the sea in order to pursue a sport or pastime. Most of these people will make use of a static camp. Having reached their destination they will camp in one place while they pursue their chosen activity. A static camp may not appear to be so different from a standing camp but the essential difference is, of course, that the equipment for a static camp may have to be carried for many miles into wild country before the camp is made. Mountaineers on expedition usually have to combine mobile and static camping. The walk into the mountain area may take days or even weeks, moving camp each day. Once the mountain is reached a static base camp is made and from here smaller mobile camps are established as the climbers ascend the mountain.

Whatever form of lightweight camping you prefer, the basic principles are common to all. In the following pages you will find all the essential information to enable you, with a little practice, to get out and camp with friends of your own age. To be self-reliant and to remain warm, dry, comfortable and well-fed in any weather conditions is not easy. It takes something which this book cannot give you, experience. This can only be gained by going out and camping as often as possible. There are times when things will go wrong and you will perhaps be wet, cold and miserable, but these experiences, unpleasant though they may be at the time, will teach you more about camping than weeks of perfect weather. If you can emerge from the less pleasant experiences still smiling and having learned something about why things went wrong you will soon gain the confidence to extend your activities to all seasons of the year. At this stage you will be a seasoned camper, strong, capable and self-reliant, and the freedom of the wilds will be yours.

CHAPTER TWO
Choosing Your Tent

One weekend many years ago two of my friends arrived with a brand-new mountain tent. It was their pride and joy and we were all very envious. That night it rained very hard and we spent a rather uncomfortable night in our old tent. The next morning, with the rain still falling steadily, we made our way across to the new mountain tent, expecting to find the occupants dry and snug. Imagine our surprise upon finding two miserable figures huddled in the back of the tent to avoid the large pool of water which occupied the whole of the front, while the rain continued to beat in through the canvas! The reason was that they had chosen the wrong tent for the job. Although it was expensive, strong and well made it was designed to be used at high altitude and was snowproof but not waterproof.

Just as an animal living in the wild will take great care about choosing its home, what it will be made of, what size and shape it will be and where it will be situated, so must you take equal care when choosing your home for camping in the wilds. Selecting the right tent can be a very difficult business as the beginner is faced with such a bewildering variety from which to choose. Before buying a tent you should try to answer the following basic questions:

1. How much can I afford to spend? The old saying 'Buy cheap, buy twice' is as true of camping equipment as it is of most other things. In general you get what you pay for, so try to get the best you can afford but make sure that you are not paying for expensive refinements which you are perhaps unlikely to need.

2. How many people will it have to accommodate? Tents for lightweight camping are sold as one-, two- or three-man, the most popular size being

two-man. Beyond these numbers you need to think in terms of two or more tents, as the larger tents are designed for purely standing camps and are too heavy and bulky to be carried around in a rucksack. At the other extreme a one-man tent is not a good idea unless you intend to do a lot of solo mobile camping, intend to cover long distances each day and wish to travel light. One-man tents are usually very small and cramped and difficult to live comfortably in for any length of time. When you are camping for periods longer than an overnight stay a little extra space makes a lot of difference to comfort.

3. Where, and when, do you intend to use your tent? As we have already seen, a tent made for use in the mountains may not be ideal in a lowland situation. Modern mountain tents are usually waterproof but they are very specialized and tend to be heavy, cramped and expensive. For most camping in summer conditions any standard tent will suffice and can also be used for the occasional high camp in settled weather conditions. If you intend to camp throughout the winter, however, your tent will have to be able to withstand violent storms, wind, rain and snow, and should therefore above all be strong. Summer storms are not uncommon in Britain but are not usually so frequent or so violent as those of winter. If you do get things wet in a summer storm you can usually dry them out shortly afterwards. This is not so in winter.

4. Will it be mainly used for mobile or static camping? A tent for mobile camping will have to be carried on your back all day and should be as light as possible yet still strong and waterproof. Good quality ultra-lightweight tents are usually quite expensive. A tent which is mainly to be used for static camping can be of heavier construction.

Choosing Your Tent

The above questions cover the most important factors which will influence your choice of tent, but there are others. Before we consider these it will be necessary to familiarize yourself with the parts of a tent which are common to all and the variations which exist.

The material from which the tent is made will determine its weight to a large extent. The majority of tents for lightweight camping are made from closely woven cotton which, in itself, is not waterproof. It has to be treated with a waterproofing agent, usually a wax or silicone wax solution. This is done by the manufacturer but after a few years' use you may find it necessary to reproof the tent yourself. This is quite easily done using a proprietary brand of proofing solution obtainable at any camping shop. Very lightweight tents, mainly intended for mobile camping, are now usually made of proofed nylon. Despite its apparent flimsiness proofed nylon is very strong and very waterproof. When the proofing does cease to be effective, however, it is not possible to reproof it yourself, the material is rather more noisy than cotton in the wind, and it is easily damaged by contact with hot objects, as nylon has a low melting point.

What we term a tent really consists of three parts: a tent, a flysheet and a groundsheet. The *tent* is the part in which you live, and its shape is determined largely by the type and number of poles which support it. Fig. 1 shows a typical ridge tent. The *groundsheet*, as the name implies, is a waterproof sheet which goes on the ground inside the tent. Even in a very dry summer a groundsheet is essential. Many tents have groundsheets permanently sewn into place; this makes the tent more windproof and slightly easier to pitch but it is by no means essential or even desirable for inexperienced campers. A separate groundsheet can be taken out to be

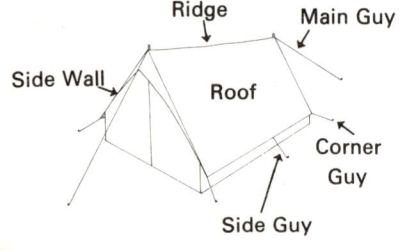

Fig. 1 Ridge tent

cleaned and can be easily replaced if damaged. It can also be turned back to allow water to escape or to cover up other equipment if the tent should leak in heavy rain. A good groundsheet can be made quite cheaply from a piece of heavy duty plastic sheet. I used to use a plastic tablecloth in one of my first tents! When you are mobile-camping it can also be useful to carry the tent and groundsheet separately and thus divide the load more equally between two or three people.

Proofed cotton is not entirely waterproof. When it rains the water is held by its surface tension within the fibres of the cotton. If the surface tension is broken by someone touching the tent at one point the water will begin to drip through. When you are living in a small tent in wet weather it is very difficult to avoid touching the walls and so getting the inside of the tent wet. Skilful campers are usually able to achieve this, but having to avoid the walls makes the interior seem even smaller and movement is very restricted in wet weather. The answer, for any serious camping in the British Isles, is to use a *flysheet* (fig. 2). This is really a second tent over the first one. The flysheet must not touch the tent and is kept clear by the poles and guys.

The advantages of a flysheet are obvious. Rain is prevented from hitting the tent and so the occupants can move about without fear of touching the walls. A flysheet also helps to keep the tent a little cooler in sunny weather and provides extra storage space beneath the eaves. Flysheets add considerably to the weight and cost of a tent but the gains in all-weather comfort are considerable. Most modern flysheets come right down to the ground, which is better in a wind and gives maximum protection to the tent. Many manufacturers now produce what are known as 'Unit' tents.

Fig. 2 Ridge tent with flysheet. Note that the extended (bell) end of the flysheet at the rear makes a guy line at this end unnecessary

Fig. 3 Single pole and 'A' pole

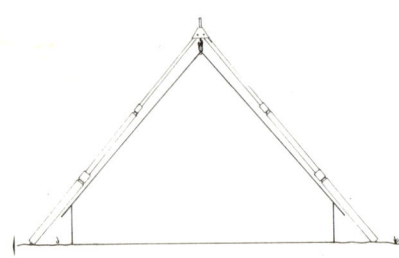

Fig. 4 Tent supported by outside 'A' pole

Choosing Your Tent

These consist of a tent, flysheet and sewn-in groundsheet sold, *and intended to be used*, as one unit. To reduce costs the tent is usually made of poorer-quality material than the flysheet and cannot be used by itself. Unit tents are often good value for money but do have the disadvantage that should you wish to make the occasional lightweight journey you cannot leave the flysheet behind to save weight.

The *poles* are the skeleton of the tent; they support it and give it strength to resist the wind. There are two main types of pole; single poles and 'A' poles (fig. 3). They can both be fitted internally, in which case the tent rests on the pole, or externally, when the tent hangs from the pole. Normally, however, single poles are fitted internally and 'A' poles externally as this gives fewer design problems. All poles for lightweight tents come apart into small sections for carrying and are made from aluminium alloy in all but the cheapest tents.

The simplest and lightest poles are single poles. When fitted inside a tent the tip of the pole is fitted into a small hole in the roof which is protected by a sewn-in metal ring called a *grommet*. Single poles have two disadvantages; they reduce the available space inside the tent and they are not so strong as 'A' poles.

'A' poles withstand windy conditions much better than single poles, and tents intended for all-the-year-round use are usually fitted with them. Most 'A' poles have a little hook at the apex and the tent hangs from this by a small loop of cord protruding from the grommet (fig. 4).

When a flysheet is used it will fit straight on to external 'A' poles which will hold it well clear of the ridge and the sides. Where a single pole is used it is necessary to fit a miniature pole, about 6 inches (150 mm) long, on to

Choosing Your Tent

the spike which protrudes through the grommet. This is known as a *separator* (fig. 5).

Some tents are supported by two poles (single or 'A' type) and are known as *ridge* tents (see fig. 1), because of the ridge formed between the two poles. A useful addition to this type of tent is a *ridge pole* which fits horizontally between the supporting poles, (fig. 6). This gives the tent increased stability and makes an excellent support for the flysheet.

Pyramid tents are supported by only one pole and all the walls slope in to a single point, rather like a wigwam (fig 7). These are the two basic tent shapes. A ridge tent is more roomy for a given height than a pyramid tent, as the area of maximum height extends for the length of the ridge. In a pyramid tent there is one central high point and it is usually difficult to sit upright except in, or close to, the centre. Ridge tents normally have the entrance on the short side while pyramid tents have it on the long side, which is very nice in summer, when plenty of ventilation may be required. Getting in and out of the tent is also much easier with a wide entrance, but in winter the smaller entrance is to be preferred as it is much easier to seal against the weather. When choosing a pyramid tent it is best to obtain one with an outside 'A' pole, as a single pole blocks the only high point in the tent. A further advantage of the 'A' pole is that, in wet weather, the tent can be unhooked and packed beneath the flysheet, which will still be supported by the pole. This can also be done with a ridge tent with outside 'A' poles but not quite so easily.

Within the basic designs there are a lot of variations, particularly in ridge tents. The more common ones are:

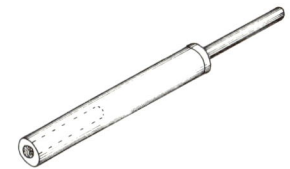

Fig. 5 Separator

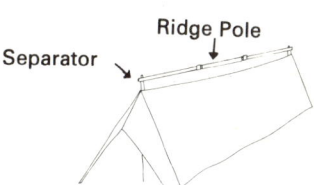

Fig. 6 Ridge pole

Fig. 7 Pyramid tent

Fig. 8 Ridge tent with bell end

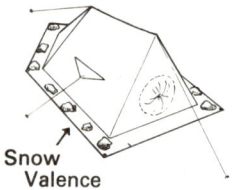

Fig. 9 Mountain tent with sleeve entrance (closed)

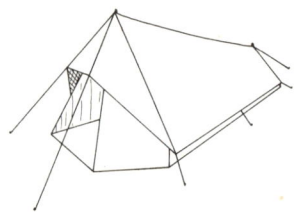

Fig. 10 Wedge tent

Choosing Your Tent

a) Ridge tent with a 'Bell' end (fig. 8). The bell end gives extra room for storing equipment etc., very useful when on a camping holiday.

b) Mountain tent (fig. 9). This is basically a strong ridge tent with small or no side walls, an arrangement which helps it to withstand high winds but reduces the space inside. 'A' poles are standard and these often fit into sleeves to increase the stability in high winds.

c) Wedge tents (fig. 10). These are designed to save weight and bulk and to withstand wind better when the smaller end is pitched directly into it. They tend to be rather cramped and it is necessary to sleep with your head to the door. (Most experienced campers sleep with feet to the door.) Wedge tents are useful when you are mobile-camping and weight is an important factor but are too cramped for really comfortable camping over a long period.

d) Pyramid tent with an extended flysheet (fig. 11). This is an excellent design for summer static camping. It is very roomy and you can safely cook under the large extension in wet weather. It is, however, bulky and heavy and does not stand up too well to strong winds.

The most popular all-round general-purpose design is probably the ridge tent with a bell end, as you can live comfortably in it for any length of time and it can also be occasionally used for the more specialized aspects of camping.

You will find that tents have quite a wide variety of *entrances*, most of which will be satisfactory for summer camping. Nobody has yet designed the perfect entrance; it has to be easy to open and close, be windproof and snowproof, provide maximum space for entrance and exit, and give good ventilation when required. Many tents now have zip fastening entrances, which is a good compromise with the one disadvantage that zips can get jammed or broken quite easily and it is then difficult to fasten or unfasten the door. This can be a nuisance if you are camping for a long period and a new zip cannot be readily obtained or fitted. The older systems using tie-tapes or press-studs, if well designed with a good overlap between the two doors, are quite adequate for summer camping and are not prone to sudden failure. Many mountain tents have sleeve entrances which are like little tunnels (fig. 12). These are excellent for keeping out wind and snow but difficult to get in and out of and are unnecessary for summer and lowland camping.

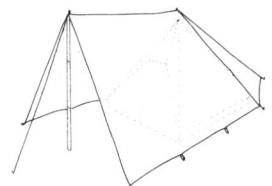

Fig. 11 Extended flysheet fitted to pyramid tent

The amount of room which you have inside your tent will be determined to a certain extent by the size of the *side walls*. A tent with high side walls will have more room than one of similar length and width but with low side walls (fig. 13). You will also notice that the higher the side wall the shallower the angle of the roof. The angle of the roof is known as the *pitch* and determines how well the tent will shed water when it rains. A steeply pitched roof sheds rain well and (because the side wall is small) offers less resistance to wind but will give a less roomy tent.

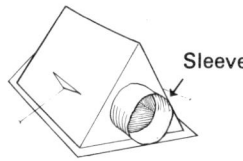

Fig. 12 Sleeve entrance (open)

Some tents, particularly if designed for winter use, have a strip of material about 9 inches (225 mm) wide around the base on the outside. This is known as a *snow valence* or boulder flap (see fig. 9). On to this can be piled snow or small rounded boulders to help keep the base of the tent down in a wind. When you are doing this the boulders should not be placed too close to the wall, otherwise the canvas flapping against them will quickly wear into a hole. Last but by no means least, we must consider *guy lines* and *tent pegs*. Without these the tent would not stay

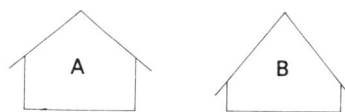

Fig. 13 Effect of high side walls. Tent 'A' with high side walls is more roomy than tent 'B' but 'B' will shed water better because of the steeper roof

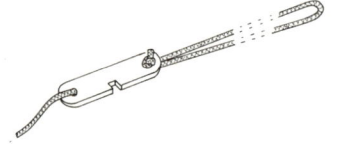

Fig. 14 Slider. The guy line can be prevented from slipping by twisting it into the small notch on the side of the slider

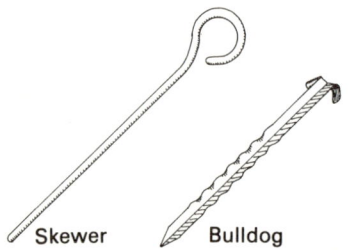

Fig. 15 Skewer and Bulldog tent pegs

upright or keep its correct shape. Guy lines are best made of braided terylene or nylon cord and their length can be adjusted by sliders (fig. 14). They are attached to the canvas by 'D' rings which are sewn on and are secured to the ground by the tent pegs. The main guys support the poles, and there are usually two of these at each end of the ridge, as they take the main strains imposed on the tent by the wind. The main job of side and corner guys is to hold the tent out into its correct shape and to prevent the canvas flapping in the wind. There are basically two types of tent peg, skewer and bulldog (fig. 15). The latter give a better hold in all types of ground but are heavier. It is a sound practice to use bulldog pegs for those guys which take the most strain, such as the main and side guys, particulary on the flysheet, and skewers for all the rest. Alloy skewer pegs are considerably lighter than steel but add to the expense. Bulldogs are usually made of steel.

With all this information at your fingertips you should now be able to answer the following questions:

What type and shape of tent do I want?
Which type of pole is best suited to my needs?
What sort of doorway is best?
Do I need a sewn-in groundsheet?
Do I require a tent with or without a flysheet?
What special design features do I require?

Having answered the four basic questions and bearing the above considerations in mind you should now have a very good idea of the type of tent which you require. You next have to obtain a selection of makers' catalogues (from camping shops or through advertisements in camping and climbing magazines), pick out the tents which meet your requirements in the different catalogues and compare their features and prices. Try to see the tent of your choice erected if at all possible. It is often difficult to get an idea of the size of a tent from a set of measurements. If you can hire one or use a friend's before making a final decision so much the better. If you know any experienced campers, find out what tents they use and recommend but do not be entirely influenced by their views, as their main requirements for a tent may be different from your own. The more information you can gather about the tents in which you are interested the better your chances of spending your money wisely.

A new tent requires a little time for the canvas to age. New canvas will tend to let a little rain through in a fine spray until the fibres swell and it is therefore a good idea to leave a new tent pitched on the lawn for two or three days before it is first used. This is not so important with nylon tents, which rely on a layer of proofing for their waterproof qualities.

CHAPTER THREE
Pitching and Striking

The more efficiently you can pitch (erect) and strike (take down) your tent the better it will be when you have to do it in bad conditions, rain and wind. Practise at home until you can do it easily. In fact it is a good idea to spend a night camping at home on the lawn, doing your own cooking and discovering some of the problems, before you spend a real night out in the wilds on your own or with a friend.

When pitching a tent your aim should be to get it up quickly and firmly. The longer it lies on the ground the wetter it will become if it is raining, and a very wet tent will leak. Using the following method you can pitch a tent single-handed if necessary, although the task will be completed more quickly if there are two of you. The method described is for a ridge tent but applies equally to pyramid tents, which are, in fact, slightly easier to erect.

1. Before unpacking anything choose your site carefully. (For details of this see chapter 6.)
2. Assemble the poles, keeping the tent rolled up in order to keep it dry for as long as possible if raining, and place them ready for use. Some poles are connected with a piece of cord which makes them easy to assemble and still allows them to fold for carrying. You can easily fit such a cord to your poles. It is only necessary to drill a small hole in the top and bottom sections to secure the cord when threaded (fig. 16). When the poles are assembled, take out the tent pegs and make sure that the peg, pole and tent bags are securely packed away if it is a windy day.
3. Unroll the tent and peg the base to the ground with the back of the tent pointing into the wind (fig. 17).
4. Fit the back pole, stand the back of the tent upright and peg out the

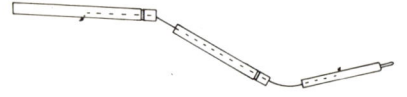

Fig. 16 Pole sections connected by cord

back main guy lines. The slider should be adjusted so that about a quarter of the total length is doubled. This applies to all guys and allows a good range of further adjustment. The back of the tent will now stand up by itself, as the guys will hold it against the wind (fig. 18).

Fig. 17 *Tent erection 1. Tent laid out with the base pegged into position, back into the wind*

Pitching and Striking

Fig. 18 Tent erection 2. Back pole erected. Note how the guy line supports it against the wind which is blowing from the rear

5. Fit the front pole and erect the front of the tent. The tent is now standing and shedding water, and you can put your rucksack inside at this stage if it is raining (fig. 19).

6. Peg out the corner guys and finally the side guys in approximately their correct positions. When they are all in place it may be necessary to move one or two slightly to get the tent to stand correctly. As a general guide each guy line should lie in line with the seam to which it is attached. When the tent is correctly positioned push the pegs right in and tension the guys (fig. 20). The canvas should be free from creases. A crease is usually

Pitching and Striking 29

Fig. 19 Tent erection 3. Both poles erected

caused by having some guys too tight and others too slack; try to work out which guys are at fault and adjust them. A little practice will soon make you efficient at removing creases.

7. If you have internal poles fit the separators; these will not be necessary with external 'A' poles. Fit the ridge pole if you have one and put the flysheet on (fig. 21). Peg out the corner guys first to ensure that the flysheet is equally spaced around the tent and then peg out the main and side guys (fig. 22). (Flysheets which come down to ground level will have elastic loops rather than guy lines.)

Pitching and Striking

Fig. 20 Tent erection 4. All guy lines pegged out. Note the ridge pole

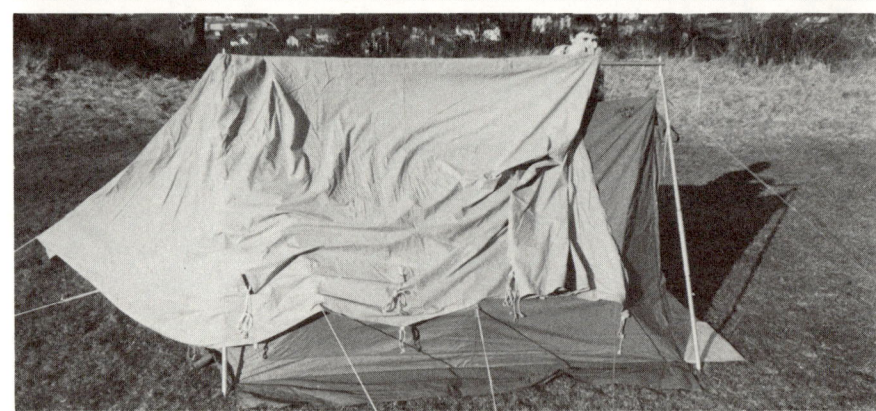

Fig. 21 Tent erection 5. Flysheet being put on

Pitching and Striking

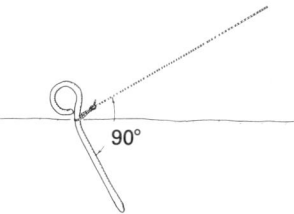

Fig. 22 Tent erection 6. Flysheet in place; it comes right down to the ground and has bell ends at the front and the back, so main guys are unnecessary

Fig. 23 Correctly placed peg

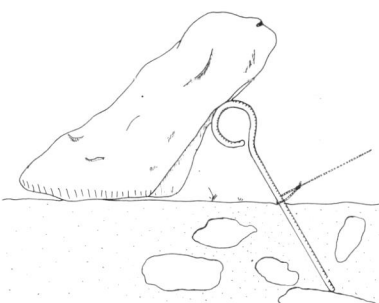

Fig. 24 Improving a poorly placed peg

When putting in tent pegs always put them at right angles to the guy lines and insert them up to the head; this is the most secure position (fig. 23). In stony ground it may not be possible to get some of the pegs in right up to the head. To increase the security put the guy line at ground level and place a large stone on the head of the peg (fig. 24). Ensure that the stone does not touch the guy or it will be likely to fray through in the wind. (This usually happens in the middle of the night when it is raining!) If you lose or break any of the pegs the guys can be tied to large stones as a temporary measure, but pad any sharp edges with moss, or the tent bag, to prevent the guy fraying. Another way is to tie the guy to a piece of wood and place stones on the wood either side. The wood will not fray the guy so easily, particularly if a rounded tree branch can be used.

Pitching and Striking

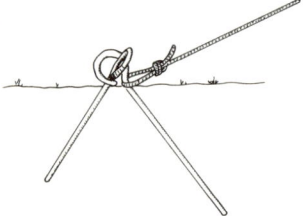

Fig. 25 Double pegging

Skewer pegs will tear out easily in soft, sandy soil. To help prevent this, use any spare pegs to double peg all the windward guys (those nearest to the direction from which the wind is blowing). This is done by pushing the extra peg through the eye of the first (fig. 25).

Pitched securely in this way your tent will stand up to very strong winds. Try to form the habit of checking all the pegs and guys each evening just before you go to bed. If any are beginning to work loose they can be re-secured at this time, which may save you a disturbed night.

Striking

Striking the tent should be carried out as systematically as pitching. Always try to strike in dry weather if at all possible; striking a wet tent in pouring rain is a miserable business.

1. Pack all your equipment into your rucksack and then wipe the inside of the groundsheet clean.
2. Take out all the flysheet pegs, starting with the sides, then the corners and finally the main guys. In firm ground it may be necessary to use a spare peg as a lever to extract the others. DO NOT pull out the pegs by pulling on the guy lines. Scrape all excess soil off the pegs as they are removed and put them together in a pile so that none are lost.
3. Double each main guy, double it again and tie it in a loose knot to prevent tangles. Side guys being shorter need only be doubled, using the slider.
4. Remove the flysheet and lay it on its side on the grass, fold the ends in

to make it into a rectangle (fig. 26), then fold it lengthways into two or three. Leave it like this while you take the tent down, unless it packs into a separate bag, in which case it can be rolled and packed away.

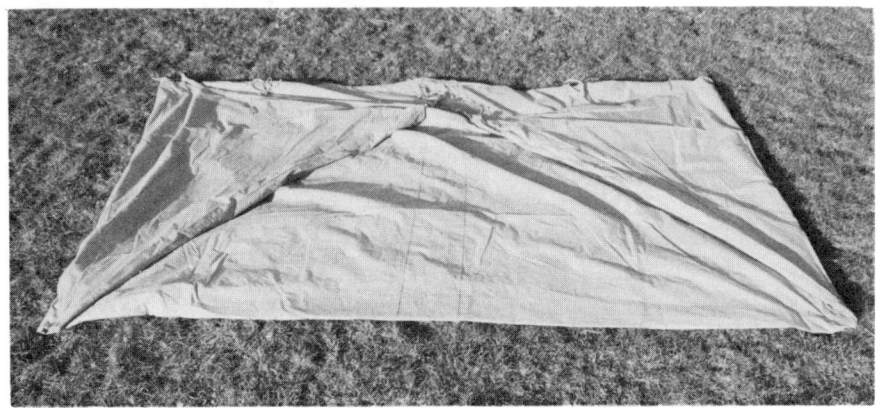

Fig. 26 Tent striking 1. Flysheet ready for folding. The bell ends have been turned in to make a rectangle

5. Remove the tent pegs in the same order as those of the flysheet and treat the guys in the same manner.
6. Turn the tent over and clean the underside of the groundsheet if it is sewn-in. If the ground is wet and muddy do this when folding the tent (see paragraph 8 below) so that the canvas does not get dirty and wet.
7. Turn the tent back again, lift the ridge by the grommets (you will find this easier to do with help) and lay it level with one of the sides of the groundsheet (fig. 27). Fold in the bell end, if fitted, to make a rectangle.

Fig. 27 Tent striking 2. Tent ready for folding. The ridge has been laid to one side and the bell end turned in to make a rectangle

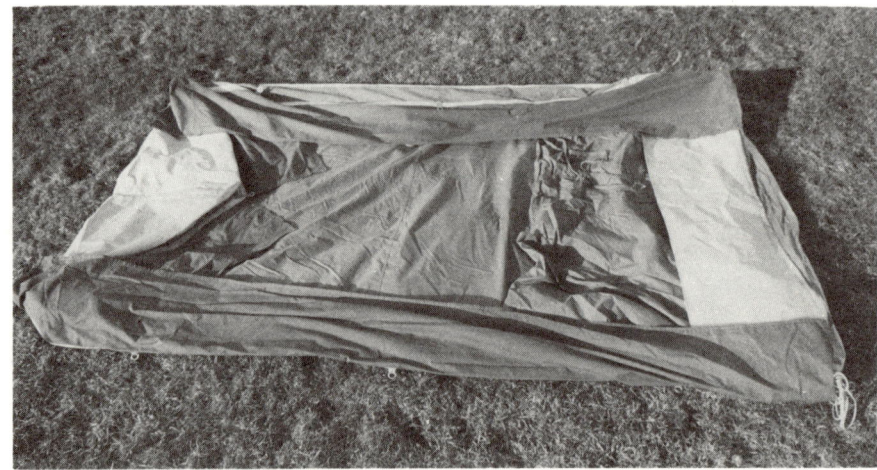

Fig. 28 Tent striking 3. Tent folded to pole width and ready to roll

8. Fold lengthways into two or three. The finished width should be equal to the length of the tent bag. (The length of a pole section will usually act as a guide.) Fold into half, lay the poles on top, roll up and place in the tent bag (fig. 28). Put the pegs into their bag heads down so that the points do not make holes in the bag. Put the peg bag carefully into the tent bag so that the points do not damage the groundsheet or tent material.

9. When you get home, wash and dry the tent pegs and straighten any bent ones. Make sure that the tent and flysheet are *absolutely* dry before packing them away. This is most important and you will find it more fully explained in Chapter 10.

The same remarks apply to buying the remainder of your equipment as to tents. It pays to buy the best you can afford. Good camping equipment is strong and serviceable and with care will last a very long time. The pans and stove which I bought twenty-seven years ago when I first started camping are still in use today and likely to last for a long time to come.

Let's take a look at the more important items which you will need to start camping. As with tents there is a bewildering variety of equipment and it is a good idea to have a clear picture of your requirements in mind before committing yourself to buying anything.

Sleeping Bags

A good night's sleep depends a great deal on a good sleeping bag. One old camper speaking in defence of sleeping bags remarked, 'I go camping to have fun and a third of that time is spent in bed'! Two things are expected of a good sleeping bag; first it should keep you warm and secondly it should be light and compact when rolled up for carrying. The very best sleeping bags are filled with 'down', the tiny soft feathers from the breast of a goose; this is very warm yet very light and will compress into a small space when the sleeping bag is rolled up. Unfortunately in recent years down has become extremely expensive and the price of a down sleeping bag is more than all but the most dedicated of winter campers will be prepared to pay. To meet the demand for a good sleeping bag at a more reasonable price many manufacturers now use synthetic fibres, terylene batt (a sort of terylene cotton wool) being very popular. Many varieties of terylene filling are being developed at present and the

CHAPTER FOUR
Other Equipment

Other Equipment

better ones will keep you nearly as warm as down, while many of the cheaper ones will be perfectly adequate for summer camping.

The greatest disadvantage of synthetic fibres is that they are springy and do not compress as well as down, and when rolled up the sleeping bag will take up more room in your rucksack. On the other hand they are much easier to wash than down bags. Any reputable camping shop should be able to show you a range of sleeping bags and advise you as to the various qualities. Some sleeping bags have a zip right round so that they can be opened up and used as a bedspread. Unless you really want a bedspread avoid this type, as a full-length zip is a cold spot which will reduce the efficiency of the sleeping bag.

It is usual to use a sheet sleeping bag inside your sleeping bag. This can be taken out and washed after each trip and ensures that the inside of your sleeping bag stays clean and fresh. Sheet sleeping bags of cotton or nylon can be bought as such or easily made from a sheet. It is worth noting that should you wish to go youth hostelling you are required to have a sheet sleeping bag to use on the hostel beds.

Insulation

When you are sleeping in a tent most of the cold comes up from the ground. Novice campers will often put their spare clothes on top of their sleeping bags for warmth when in fact they should be putting them underneath! Insulation from cold is not essential in summertime but it does make things more comfortable. You can improvise by putting bracken under the groundsheet or several layers of newspaper on top, newspaper having excellent properties of insulation. If you can afford it buy yourself a sleeping mat to lie on. A closed cell foam mat such as 'Karrimat' is the best; it does not soak up water because of its closed cell construction (therefore it can be carried on the outside of a pack), it is a very good insulator and rolls up quite small. A full-length foam mat is unnecessary. You require insulation only from shoulders to hips except in very cold winter conditions. If you cannot find a small one buy a full-length one between yourself and a friend and cut it in half.

Stoves

There are four types of camping stove commonly available: petrol, methylated spirit, gas and paraffin (fig. 29).

Fig. 29 Common types of camping stove. Left to right: petrol, methylated spirit, paraffin, gas

Other Equipment

The petrol stove has little to recommend it. The fuel is dangerous, difficult to store and carry, and expensive to buy. The stove itself is no more efficient than the other types and has no outstandingly good features not to be found in the other types.

Methylated spirit is a pleasant fuel to handle and safer than petrol but again rather expensive. Choice of methylated spirit stoves is rather limited and the best available at present is the 'Trangia' type, which includes a set of dixies, is easy to light and burns well in a wind. The actual stove is very simple and there are no washers, pumps, valves etc., to go wrong, but there are only two flame positions, high and very low, which rather limits the type of cooking you can do.

Gas stoves are easy to light but the gas cartridges do not last very long and are very expensive in comparison with other fuels. The stove does not burn well in a wind. Changing gas cylinders can be dangerous if done incorrectly. If you possess a gas stove NEVER change a cylinder inside your tent or near a flame of any kind. Both methylated spirit and gas stoves have the advantage of lightness and convenience over other types available.

Paraffin pressure stoves, known to most people as 'Primus' stoves (Primus is the trade name of a very famous make), are the choice of many experienced campers. The fuel is rather messy but cheap and easy to obtain. The stove is very robust and all spares are easily obtainable for the popular makes. (Check this before you buy.) Pressure, to give you a big flame for boiling water etc., is built up by pumping and can be released through a small valve. Thus you can control the stove to give any size of flame even when the fuel is almost used up, unlike the gas stove where the pressure drops as the fuel in the cylinder gets low. The one-pint-capacity primus is the one most widely used; one tankful of fuel should last you for a summer weekend, making it unnecessary to carry spare fuel.

Primus stoves are not so easy to erect or light as gas or methylated spirit stoves. Follow the instructions carefully and preferably get an experienced friend to help you the first time you attempt to light one. Always light the stove in a sheltered place but NOT inside the tent, and use plenty of priming fuel so that the burner gets really hot before you start pumping. Failure to get the burner sufficiently hot will result in a yellow, smoky flame and is the most common cause of difficulty when lighting.

Wood Fires

Cooking on a wood fire is fine in theory but it can be very difficult in practice. Wood is not always easily obtainable, particularly in popular camping areas, and in periods of heavy rain you will find it difficult to light a fire even if you have the wood. Even a small fire is very demanding, as once lit it needs a constant supply of wood. It also makes your pans very black and sooty indeed. When all this has been said the fact remains that there is something pleasant and exciting about cooking over a wood fire and most youngsters get a lot of fun out of it. So take a stove to do most of your cooking, but if you find a place where there is plenty of dry, dead wood and where it is safe to have a fire then you can try your hand. Do not be surprised if your first attempts are unsuccessful; there is a lot of skill involved in cooking on a wood fire! Remember that the fire should be very small and laid between level stones on which to rest your pans. Let the flames die down to hot embers and cook on those; there is more heat from

Other Equipment

embers and less smoke to blacken your pans. Site the fire downwind of the tent and well clear so that sparks will not be blown on the canvas. Make quite sure that fire lighting is permitted before you start; there are certain places and times of the year when the fire risk is very high and fires are forbidden, on forestry campsites for example. Never leave a fire alight if you go away from the camp and make sure that it is really out by dowsing it with water.

Pans

Pans, usually called dixies or billies, are sold in sets. The handles are removable or folding and the dixies stack inside each other for convenience when carrying. They are usually made of aluminium and the better quality ones are thicker and will last longer than cheap ones. Buy a good-sized set, the largest pan of which should hold three to four pints. It is a mistake to buy a very small set; the size of the larger pan governs the size of the lid/frying pan and it is easier to cook a small quantity in a large pan than vice versa. The set which you choose should also have strong, well-fitting handles. If this is not so you can buy a strong pot-lifter designed to fit most makes of dixies. Preferably obtain a steel one.

Lighting

The safest form of lighting is a torch or battery lamp which can be suspended from the highest point of the tent, and this may be all that is required in the summer when the days are long. However, torch light is not very efficient and casts a lot of shadows. The best form of lighting is the simple, old-fashioned candle but it is at the same time the most dangerous and many tent fires have been caused by careless use. If you intend to use candles observe the following precautions:

1. Buy short, thick candles or night lights; they do not fall over so easily. 'Carriage candles' or long-burning candles are good and are available from many camping and hardware stores.
2. Buy or make a candle-holder. Your candle is much safer in a holder than stuck down by wax to the top of a tin can. A simple holder can be made from a large tin lid (fig. 30) or by embedding the candle in a small tin filled with sand or earth.
3. Place the candle on a firm, level surface well away from the walls. Remember that the roof slopes in and that there should be plenty of space between the roof and the candle flame. Hold your hand against the roof above the flame. If it is too hot to keep it there the flame is too close!
4. Be careful not to knock it over if you move about.
5. NEVER leave the candle alight when you go out of the tent, even for a very short time.
6. Do not fall asleep with the candle alight. If you are reading in your sleeping bag (a favourite occupation of winter campers in the evening) blow the candle out as soon as you feel sleepy.

Remember that most tents are proofed with a wax solution and are very inflammable. Do not take chances (fig. 31).

Fig. 30 Improvised candle-holder. Cut along the dotted lines and fold back the triangular flaps thus formed to fit the candle

Other Equipment

Fig. 31 Tents are very inflammable!

Water Containers

A water container should hold at least one gallon so that you do not have to make frequent trips to the source of supply. Most popular today are plastic collapsible bottles, but these sometimes make the water taste of plastic, particularly in hot weather. Because of this some people still prefer to use a canvas water bucket. The latter folds into a very small space for carrying and the water stays cooler in hot weather, owing to evaporation, but it can be easily knocked over when in use. Canvas water buckets are now sometimes difficult to obtain.

Rucksacks

Any large rucksack will suffice to begin with, but if you have to buy one choose it with care, as it is a long-term investment. Basically there are three types: frameless, frame and packframe. For carrying heavy loads such as camping gear most people consider a frame rucksack to be slightly better than a frameless, but a frame sack is heavier, so it is largely a matter of preference. A good compromise is the half-frame sack, which looks as though it is frameless but has a certain amount of stiffening built into the back. Packframes (fig. 32) consist of an aluminium frame on to which one can strap a load of any shape, even a packing case. Most packframes can be bought with a sack designed to fit them. You can, if you (or your mother!) are handy with a sewing machine, buy a packframe and make a sack of your own design out of proofed nylon to fit it, or you could obtain an old army kit bag and strap that to the frame.

The points to look for in a rucksack of any kind are:

1. Strong fittings, particularly the attachment of the carrying straps.
2. A large lid fitted with long fastening straps.
3. Big side pockets fitted high on the sack.
4. The sack should be wedge-shaped, wider at the top than the bottom.

Fig. 32 Packframe with home-made fitted sack. Note the side lacing which can be used to alter the capacity of the sack

Other Equipment

5. Strong material, preferably waterproof.
6. The correct size. Most good rucksacks are now made in several sizes. Make sure that you get the right one for you, as it is hard work carrying a sack which is too large or too small.

If you study the camping checklists in Chapter 11 you will find a lot of minor items. Many of these may be improvised or borrowed from the kitchen (knives, forks etc.) but make sure that you bring them back. Your mother will not appreciate the loss of a set of cutlery every time you go camping!

CHAPTER FIVE

Packing Your Rucksack

You are all ready to set out on your first camping trip and all your food and equipment is assembled on the floor. The pile looks immense and there does not seem to be any possibility that it will all go into one rucksack, yet go it must, and it will if you set about it in the right way.

There are two principles to bear in mind when packing any rucksack. First, always try to pack so that the weight is high up near your shoulders; this keeps the centre of gravity close to your body (fig. 33). If you have all the weight down at the bottom as in an old-fashioned or badly packed rucksack you have to lean forward a lot, which soon makes your back ache and walking uncomfortable. The second principle is that you always pack last the things which you are going to need first when you get to camp.

Now you are ready to start. First line your rucksack with a large polythene bag; a dustbin bag is ideal. All else goes into this, which will keep things dry should your rucksack leak. Do not assume that your rucksack will be absolutely waterproof even if it is new. Now roll up your sleeping bag as tightly as possible, put it in another polythene bag (take no chances with your sleeping bag, it must stay dry), and squash it down into the bottom of your rucksack. You are not going to need it until evening and it is fairly light, so that satisfies both principles. Although you have squashed your sleeping bag tightly into your rucksack there will still be small spaces around the bottom. Fill them up now; you will not be able to reach them later on. Push in small, soft, light objects such as handkerchiefs, spare socks etc. When you have got as much around the sleeping bag as you can, put in the remainder of your spare clothing. Now you can start inserting the heavier items. Put the stove in first, if it is a primus,

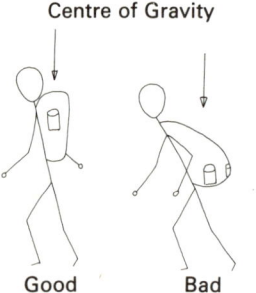

Fig. 33 *Load carrying. The high load (left) keeps the centre of gravity much closer to the spine*

making sure that the safety valve, filler cap and burner cap are firmly fastened to prevent paraffin leaking over everything. If you have a gas stove, check that it is properly turned off. As an added precaution you can also enclose the stove in a polythene bag. Next to the stove place the dixies but do not leave them empty; that is a waste of valuable space. Fill them with small odds and ends such as candles, matches, butter etc. This is a good place to carry eggs if you intend to take them. Wrap each one in newspaper and pack them in carefully, they will survive a lot of rough handling if packed in this way. Around the stove and dixies pack the remainder of your food, your mug (fill that also) and any remaining odds and ends. Fold your sleeping mat to fit into the top (or it can be strapped outside if you are short of space), pack your anorak and over-trousers next so that they are easily reached should it rain on the walk in, then fasten up the mouth of your rucksack with the drawcord. As you gain experience you will develop your own ideas about packing and where you prefer to have individual items, but the above is a good basis to work on.

Into one side pocket put your container of spare paraffin. Always use the same pocket for this and do not put anything into that pocket which could be spoiled by the taint of paraffin, such as a cream cake for your tea! Try to ensure that your paraffin container does not leak but in any case enclose it in a polythene bag. Use the other side pocket for things which you may need on the journey: camera, lunch and plasters in case of blisters if you are not used to walking. Always stop and put a plaster on as soon as your heel starts to feel sore; it is easier to prevent a blister than to cure one! If your rucksack flap has a zip pocket you can also use this for items which you might require on the journey. Finally, the heaviest item and the one

Packing Your Rucksack

which you are going to need first, the tent, is placed on top of the sack and the flap buckled over to hold it into place.

Your rucksack should now look something like that in fig. 34. If you have packed it well there should be no unused spaces and nothing except the tent fastened to the outside. It will probably feel very heavy at first until you get used to carrying it. Of course, if you are camping with friends you will be able to split up all communal gear such as stove, dixies, tent and food between you and thus lighten your load. As a general rule your rucksack should not weigh more than a third of your own weight when fully packed; i.e. if you weigh 90 lb (41 Kg) your rucksack should not weigh more than 30 lb (13.7 Kg). If your rucksack ever weighs more than about 25 lb (11.5 KG) without food it means that you must be carrying some unnecessary weight. Have a good look through and see what you can leave behind – the odd can of lemonade, perhaps!

It does not take many camping trips to make you very weight-conscious. The first time I ever went camping I took, amongst several other superfluous items, two pint bottles of milk. By the following weekend I had substituted one small tin of condensed milk! You will soon learn by experience exactly what you need to take and what luxuries you are prepared to carry in addition to the essentials.

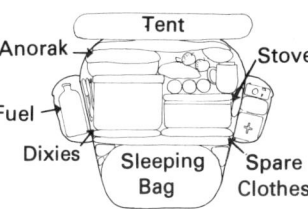

Fig. 34 A well-packed rucksack

CHAPTER SIX

Choosing a Campsite

The walk in was enjoyable, but the rucksack felt rather heavy and you were glad to stop for a breather a couple of times on the way. Now you have arrived at your destination with your neck and shoulder muscles aching (never mind, they will grow stronger with practice) and you are happy to put the rucksack down while you look around for a suitable place for the tent. Take your time, the sun is shining and there is no hurry. A lot may depend on being in just the right place should the weather deteriorate. There are four important things to bear in mind when choosing a place for a tent; let's take a look at them in order of priority

1. **Shelter** (fig. 35)

Strong wind is the greatest enemy of tents, a tent exposed to the full force of a gale is not going to stay up very long unless it is an exceptional tent. Some kind of shelter must be found, but first you need to know the most likely direction from which the wind will come. In most places in the British Isles the prevailing wind (the wind which blows most of the time) blows from the south west. This is where the gales and really bad weather will usually come from, but it may vary locally, owing perhaps to the shape of the valley. Take a look at the trees round about. Which way do they lean? Will they lean into the wind or away from it? You are right, they will lean away. What can we find for shelter? Anything which will break the force of the wind will suffice, a high stone wall, a large boulder, a thick hedgerow or a group of trees. Yes, over there, a grove of trees in just the right place. You should not place the tent beneath the trees because, after rain, water will continue to drip from the leaves and branches long after the rain has stopped, but you need to be close enough to get shelter. Let's go over and see if it satisfies our other requirements.

2. **Dry Ground** (fig 36)

By dry ground we mean ground which will be reasonably dry after a period of heavy rain. Even fairly flat ground will have slight bumps and hollows and in heavy rain the hollows may fill with water, so we must try to avoid them. Have a good look at the grass too. Can you see any marsh plants, mosses or reeds in it? If you can it is likely to be fairly boggy when wet.

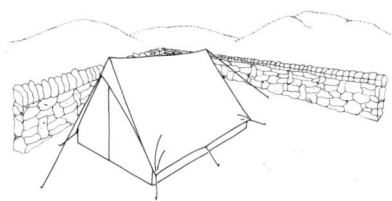

Fig. 35 Shelter. The angle of two walls will often provide good shelter from the wind

3. **Flat Ground**

Preferably the ground should be flat – not too difficult to find in the lowlands but it can be a problem in the hills. Sloping ground can make sleeping more difficult and it may be harder to place the stove securely. If you do have to pitch on a slight slope make sure that you position the tent so that your head will be uphill when you go to sleep. Do not pitch across the slope; you will spend the night rolling on your companion or being rolled upon. If you are ever forced to pitch across a slope by lack of space make sure that you sleep on the uphill side, it's much the more comfortable position.

Fig. 36 Avoid hollows!

Well, the ground just in the lee of the trees is quite flat and grassy and it does not look as though it is likely to be marshy, so this could be the best place for the tent. There is one more thing to consider and that is:

4. Water Supply

Preferably your water supply should be within easy reach of the tent. It is no good having a nice, sheltered, flat, dry spot about half a mile (1 kilometre) from the water supply if it is raining hard. Be careful about streams; they may look sparkling and pure but looks can be deceptive. As a good general rule do not drink stream water if there are houses upstream. If there is no upstream habitation, walk along the stream for about 100 yards/metres just to make sure that there is nothing nasty, such as a dead sheep, lying in it. Spring water is usually pure and safe to drink, especially if you are able to collect it near to its source.

Unless you know the water to be pure, i.e. tap water or that which the local people drink themselves, always boil it before drinking. This will kill the majority of harmful bacteria likely to be present. If you are camping on farm land or on an official camp site ask the farmer or owner where the supply of drinking water is to be found.

Once you have carefully chosen your site, erect the tent as described in Chapter 3. If you have already practised this at home you should have no trouble. Before you lay the groundsheet down check to ensure that there are no stones or other objects underneath which may damage it and also give you an uncomfortable night. Take your time and make sure that the tent is standing firmly with all the pegs securely placed.

CHAPTER SEVEN
Living In Your Tent

To live comfortably and happily in a small tent for any length of time demands a certain amount of careful planning and organization. People who go off on expeditions to the wild places of the world often have to live in tents for two or three months, sometimes in difficult weather conditions. If they were not skilful and well organized they would have a very miserable time. Anyone can camp in discomfort and squalor; the art lies in being able to make yourself comfortable whatever the circumstances, and this is what you should aim for. Every time you camp, even if only overnight, tackle it as though you were preparing for a long stay. At the end of each trip ask yourself the question 'Could I have stayed another night?' If the answer is 'No', try to discover the reason and how you can prevent it happening the next time. In this way you will quickly learn from your experiences and will soon become an expert camper with the ability to stay warm, snug, dry and well-fed in any conditions.

Once your tent is erected you can unpack your rucksack and arrange your kit. If you have foam-mats or other insulation place these in position first. If the weather is fine your sleeping bag can be taken out, unrolled, loosely folded and placed near the back of the tent. This gives the filling a chance to expand and recover from being compressed in your rucksack. In very wet weather it may be advisable to keep your sleeping bag in its polythene bag until needed. The stove can now be placed near the door along with the dixies. Keep matches in a small polythene bag in the stove container along with the prickers for the stove and the candles. If you get used to keeping matches in one place you will always be able to find them, even in the dark. Food and all the odds and ends can be placed along the walls of the tent or up in the bell end. Keep the food which you intend to use first near the stove, along with the tea, sugar, milk, pepper and salt. If you are camping with a friend it is usual to keep all your personal things, washing kit, books etc. on one side of the tent while he keeps his on the other.

When your rucksack is empty it can be folded and put at the head of your foam-mat to form the basis of a pillow. This can then be built up with your spare clothes and/or the clothes which you take off at night. A surprisingly comfortable pillow can be made in this way if you arrange your clothes carefully with soft things such as sweaters on the top.

Stand your spare fuel container outside the tent, underneath the flysheet if you have one. If you are camping for several days and are short of space, things which are not really affected by rain, such as tinned foods, can also be stored under the flysheet, preferably in polythene bags because if they get very wet and all the labels fall off you will have problems! Fill your water container and place it outside the tent within easy reach but in a place where it won't do any harm if it gets knocked over.

I have just described the way in which I would organize my tent; other people may do things differently. The important thing is for you to work out a system which suits you and stick to it so that you can always be sure of finding things when you need them. There is nothing more irritating than arriving back at your tent after dark and being unable to find the torch or matches.

Cooking

The ability to provide yourself with a good, hot meal is important to your well-being when camping. First you have to plan your meals, decide what you are going to eat and how much food you require. This will depend largely on what you like to eat and on what you are capable of cooking. Try to stick to simple things at first and remember that on a camping stove you can cook only one thing at a time. Therefore elaborate meals which demand lots of pans and several things cooking simultaneously are unsuitable. Fried foods such as bacon and egg are easy but best avoided if possible, as too much fried food is not good for you and also it is very difficult to prevent fat splashing the walls of the tent. Many people think that it is necessary to use mostly dried foods when camping, but this is not so. If you wish to travel light or have to carry food for several days then dried foods are very useful, as they are compact and light in weight. However, they are not usually so tasty as fresh foods and are very expensive, so if you are out only for one or two nights you can afford the extra weight involved in taking a large proportion of fresh foods.

A useful (though not essential) item of cooking equipment is a toaster (fig. 37). The best ones consist of a sheet of tin covered by wire mesh. This is put flat on the stove. The tin gets hot and toasts the bread, which is supported above the heated tin by the wire mesh. Do not buy the type which is supposed to do about four pieces at once; they do not work very well.

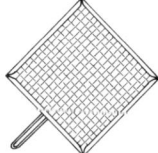

Fig. 37 Toaster

A menu for one day involving simple cooking might be as follows:
Breakfast: Boiled egg, toast, tea or coffee.
Lunch: Sandwiches, cake, fruit if away from camp or perhaps soup, bread, cake and fruit if in camp.
Dinner: Stew, cake or biscuits, tea or coffee.

Let's see how a pair of experienced campers might deal with this menu.

First a morning cup of tea. Fred keeps out of the way at the back of the tent while Bill lights the stove outside the entrance and puts the water on to boil. To save fuel he uses only the right amount of water, two mugsful plus a little to allow for evaporation. A lid on the billy helps it to boil quickly. While this is boiling he half fills a small pan with water for the eggs. When the tea water is boiling a spoonful of tea is placed into the boiling water (this is where the method differs from using a teapot), the pan is immediately lifted off the stove with the pot-lifter, the tea is stirred and left to stand for a moment. Bill puts the egg water on to boil, then pours the tea. The tea leaves have settled into the bottom of the pan and by pouring slowly and carefully (outside the tent in case of accidents) none go into the cups. Sugar and dried or condensed milk are added.

The egg water has started to boil by this time and Bill puts in the eggs. Being a wily camper he carefully pierces the shells at the pointed end with a pin just beforehand, which allows the expanding air to escape without cracking the shells. He times the eggs for four minutes and gets out two slices of bread. After three minutes he lifts the pan of eggs off the stove and leaves them to carry on cooking in the water while he makes the toast.

While all this has been going on Fred has not been sitting idle but has been preparing the sandwiches for lunch and packing them into a polythene bag along with the cake and fruit. The eggs could be eaten chopped on to the toast, which does away with the necessity for an egg cup, or if they were originally packed into a cardboard egg container this could be used as an egg cup. Campers who eat a lot of boiled eggs might consider it worthwhile to take two light plastic egg cups. While breakfast is being eaten water is on the stove for a second cup of tea and as soon as this has boiled the stove is turned out to save fuel. Notice the timing and organization; there are no unnecessary delays and all the time the stove is lit it is in use.

On arrival back at the tent in the evening Fred opts to cook the meal. While he peels the potatoes, onions and carrots Bill makes a drink of tea or coffee. Fred puts about half an inch (10 mm) of water into a large pan, chops up the potatoes very small, puts them into the water, slices in the carrots and onions, adds salt and pepper and puts the pan on the stove to boil for about fifteen minutes, by which time the vegetables will be cooked. After fifteen minutes he adds a tin of stewed steak or corned beef cut into small pieces, an oxo cube and a tin of peas. (If dried peas are used these are added at the beginning.) The stew is stirred and Fred makes sure to steady the pan with the pot-lifter while doing so. Then the stove is turned down and the stew allowed to simmer for another five minutes, at the end of which time it is ready for eating. Fred dishes the stew out into two dixie lids, puts water into the pan for washing up and puts it back on to the stove to warm. After the stew is eaten Bill washes up while Fred makes a drink and gets out the biscuits.

The food which Bill and Fred took with them was not particularly light in weight, and if they had wished to carry food for several days it would have been necessary to use more lightweight dried foods. They chose their food because it was easy to cook, because they liked it (very important) and also because the cooking could be accomplished with only a few pans and one stove. With a little help from your mother I am sure that you can think of several such menus. If you are unused to camp cooking it is a very good idea to cook one or two meals at home on your camping stove to familiarize yourself with the techniques.

Cooking is fun but it can be dangerous. Here are some safety rules to remember:

Fig. 38 Canvas windshield

1. Cook outside the tent. If you have an extended flysheet this will give you shelter from the wind. If not, a folding, canvas windbreak can be made or bought (fig. 38). Do not try to cook in a wind; it is very slow and wasteful of fuel, as the wind takes the heat away from the pan. Make sure that the stove is well away from the flysheet and doorway.
2. Always turn the stove out and allow it to cool a little before refilling it. This should be done outside the tent.
3. Be very careful when you have things boiling on the stove, as you can be badly scalded if a pan is accidentally upset. This is why Fred sat at the back out of the way while Bill cooked breakfast. If you need to stir anything hold the dixie steady with the pot-lifter or lift it off the stove.
4. Before pumping the stove to increase pressure remove any dixie which may be on it.

Camping in Wet Weather

This is when your ability as a camper is really put to the test. Summer camping in dry weather is easy and nothing could be more pleasant, but when the rain is pouring down for hours on end, perhaps coupled with a high wind, camping skill is tested to the full. You will probably, over the years, develop your own solutions to the problems of keeping yourself and your equipment dry, but here are a few basic tips which are generally accepted by the majority of campers.

If you have chosen your site with care there should be little danger of water flooding in at ground level, but it can happen at times. When it does you may have to cut a channel to lead the water away from the tent. One sees many campsites disfigured by such channels which have been hastily and thoughtlessly hacked out, perhaps with a sharp stone. If you make two parallel knife cuts in the turf about 2 inches (50 mm) apart and about the same deep you can lift out a strip of turf which can then be placed alongside the channel on the side nearest the tent to act as an extra barrier (fig. 39). When you leave, the turf can be replaced and should grow back to leave no unsightly scars or damage.

As previously mentioned, a flysheet makes camping in wet weather much more comfortable, but if you do not have a flysheet you have to be extremely careful about touching the tent sides, so try to keep movement to a minimum. Even with a flysheet you can have problems if a strong wind keeps pushing it against the tent. If you touch the side, water will start to drip through at that point. Put your finger on the drip, press hard and run your finger down to the eave. Surprisingly the water does not start to drip through along the track of your finger but runs along it and will then drip or run down the wall, where it is not so much of a nuisance. If your groundsheet is not sewn-in it can be turned back to allow the water to drip on to the grass. If your tent should start to leak in several places, even only small drips, get your sleeping bag, spare clothes etc. into polythene bags and into your rucksack. Once your sleeping bag gets really wet it is difficult to dry it out, so try to prevent this happening at all costs.

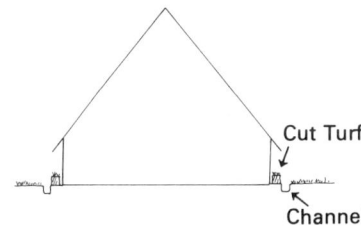

Fig. 39 Drainage channel

On arriving back at the tent in wet weather try to avoid taking water inside with you. Strip off your wet outer garments and put them under the flysheet in a polythene bag, remove your boots (as you should always do on entering a tent) and remove your socks too if they are wet. Once inside try to keep trips in and out to a minimum, so make sure that you have plenty of drinking water handy and that all the pegs and guy lines are secure before removing your outer garments and getting in.

If you are very wet take off your wet things, put on your spare clothes and put your wet things into a polythene bag. Do not leave them lying about the tent where they may make other things damp. If the rain stops you can hang them up to dry, but if you have no opportunity to do this you must PUT YOUR WET THINGS BACK ON before going out the following morning. It is not very pleasant to put on wet things, but if the weather has cleared they will soon warm up and dry out; if it is still raining it is not going to make much difference. Leaving your spare set of dry clothing on is a mistake. If it rains again you are going to have two wet sets of clothing and nothing to change into, as you cannot afford the weight or space to carry more than one spare set of clothes on a camping trip. Contrary to popular belief you will not catch your death of cold by putting on wet clothes if you are going to be active! Of course, if you intend to stay in the tent you can keep your dry clothes on.

Take every opportunity to dry things. A string stretched along the ridge inside the tent from pole to pole is useful to dry small items such as socks, pants and handkerchiefs. When the rain stops hang all your wet things up to dry (you can spread them on the hedge as the gipsies do), open the tent doors fully to allow the air to circulate and wipe up any surface moisture on the groundsheet. In unsettled weather keep an eye open for sudden showers, or your drying clothes may become much wetter!

Waste Disposal and Camp Hygiene

What you do with your rubbish is important. Many thousands of people camp in Britain each year; some are careless and irresponsible and we see the signs of this in unsightly litter in our beautiful places. Fortunately the majority of people care about the countryside and deal with their rubbish in a sensible way. If this were not so, many of our best camping spots would now be completely spoiled and it is up to all of us to do all we can to preserve the countryside so that others may enjoy it as we have done.

Waste disposal is really quite simple; take it home with you. If you can carry full tins, bottles etc. out with you it is quite easy to carry them home empty and put them in the dustbin. Any dry paper waste can be burned and tins can be flattened and put into a polythene bag. Some things can be taken out of their tins at home before leaving for camp and put into polythene bags, thus making your load lighter and reducing the amount of waste which you have to carry back. If you are on a mobile lightweight camping holiday the temptation to leave waste behind is greatest but don't succumb to it! If someone has arranged to meet you en route with fresh supplies of food they can take away your waste at the same time. If you are buying food en route you will surely find a waste-bin in the village where you make your purchases.

Official campsites will have waste disposal, washing facilities and toilets, but your camp in the wilds will have none of these things. When you need to relieve yourself you must bear two things in mind: first, don't go anywhere near the water supply or you will contaminate it for yourself and others and, secondly, leave no trace of where you have been. Dig a small hole in the topsoil and cover it over again when you have finished. The bacteria in the soil will break down the faeces, leaving no trace. Always try to get well away from the campsite into an area where nobody is likely to camp.

When washing and cleaning your teeth remember that there may be other campers further downstream, so do not wash directly in the stream and avoid throwing your soapy water in when you have finished. It will not be appreciated by other campers or by the fish!

CHAPTER EIGHT
Bivouacs and Shelters

A bivouac is basically a night out without a tent, and a planned bivouac can be great fun and an exciting adventure. Apart from the excitement of sleeping under the stars people usually bivouac to save carrying the extra weight of a tent if they wish to travel light. I have often bivouacked just for fun or to test a new sleeping bag and on more than one occasion have awakened after a sound night's sleep to find my sleeping bag heavily covered with frost!

Mountaineers often bivouac at the foot of a big alpine climb, having walked up from the valley during the day, so that they can start climbing at first light. On a long and difficult climb it may also be necessary to bivouac on tiny ledges on the cliff face. These things are part of a mountaineer's life, but we are concerned here with bivouacking in the lowlands for the sheer fun of it and to experience the really open-air life.

For a one-night summer bivouac you can travel light, with just your sleeping bag, survival bag, torch and flask containing a hot drink or soup. Take light things to eat which require no cooking, such as sandwiches, hard-boiled eggs, biscuits, chocolate etc. You can, of course, take a stove and cooking utensils if you wish but this will all add to the weight. The ability to travel light is one of the great joys of bivouacking; movement is much easier than when walking with full camp equipment and you have the challenge of making yourself comfortable for the night with the minimum of equipment and only the sky for a roof.

Obviously for your first bivouac you will try to choose a fine night with a good weather forecast for the following day. The greatest threat to a bivouac, or 'bivvy' as most mountaineers call it, is rain, and so a virtually indispensable item of equipment is a polythene survival bag. This item can be purchased quite cheaply from any mountaineering shop and is simply a large, heavy-duty polythene bag which you can get right inside in the event of rain. As survival bags are absolutely waterproof you will get a great deal of condensation forming inside when you sleep in one. It is therefore usual to use the bag as a groundsheet unless it actually starts to rain, when it becomes necessary to climb inside, the condensation being preferable to the rain.

If you carry a survival bag and spare clothing with you when you go out walking you can, in an emergency, spend a night out without coming to any great harm, and experienced mountaineers frequently carry them as part of their survival equipment. One word of warning; do not attempt to inprovise by using a large bag off a new mattress or something of that nature. Such bags are only light-gauge polythene, thin and flexible, and could easily suffocate you. This cannot happen with a proper survival bag of relatively stiff polythene, which will not cling to your face.

Plan to bivouac in a reasonably accessible place and try to time your arrival to give you about an hour to spare before dark. This will allow you time to make yourself really comfortable. When you arrive in your chosen sleeping area look around for the best spot, bearing in mind exactly the same things as you would for normal camping; shelter and a flat, dry spot. In this case you will need to be really close to whatever you have chosen to shelter you from the wind. An overhanging slab of rock or a large fallen tree will do very nicely (fig. 40). Any gaps beneath the tree can be plugged with moss or earth to stop draughts whistling through. Of course, many other features will do just as well and you must use your ingenuity to make the best of what you have around you. In a rocky area, for example, you

Fig. 40 Bivouac under an overhang

might build a low wall of stones which need be only about 2 feet (600 mm) high to afford shelter when you are lying down.

You might consider it worthwhile to add a sleeping mat to your kit, it weighs little and adds a lot to comfort – but if you are travelling really light try to find some insulation in the form of dead bracken or leaves to put under your survival bag. You can, in fact, fill your survival bag with leaves, which makes an excellent mattress, but should it rain during the night you will have to empty them all out to get inside, during which time your sleeping bag could get quite wet.

Having prepared your bed, unroll your sleeping bag and have a hot drink. Before getting into your bag put all your food and things which you wish to keep dry into your rucksack. (The stove and cooking utensils can stay out.) If it should rain the rucksack can go into the survival bag with you. Make sure your torch is at hand, as you may need it during the night, and then you are ready for bed. It will seem strange and perhaps eerie to sleep under a canopy of stars and you may not sleep easily on that first night, but to bivouac in fine weather and wake with the first rays of the morning sun, perhaps to fish that first rise of trout in the lake, is an unforgettable experience and one which you will have no hesitation in repeating at the next opportunity.

Shelters

Shelters are really elaborate bivouacs, the idea being to arrange some sort of roof which will keep the rain off. A waterproof shelter constructed solely from natural materials is difficult to achieve and there are few places

Bivouacs and Shelters

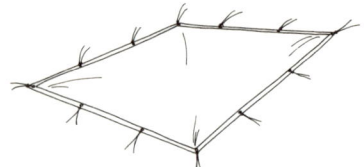

Fig. 41 Bivouac sheet

Fig. 42 Simple tent shelter

in Great Britain where you would be allowed to cut the necessary leafy branches. However, the addition of one simple item to your bivouac gear will give you a lot of scope for improvising good shelters. The required item is a piece of lightweight proofed nylon or heavy gauge polythene about 8 foot (2.5 m) square with eyelets along all edges (fig. 41). Plastic is cheap and good but the eyelets tend to tear out and it is best to tie in short lengths of cord. If you intend to use shelters often, the nylon, though more expensive, is stronger, lighter and more durable. Armed with this, some string, a few tent pegs and a certain amount of ingenuity you can make a great variety of shelters. Once you have the basic idea it is quite possible to go out for a summer lightweight walking expedition without the considerable weight of a tent to add to your load and with the added excitement of making your shelter each night, using what your surroundings have to offer.

You will quickly find all sorts of ways to utilize your shelter sheet, but here are a few basic, well-proven methods.

1. The simple tent (fig. 42). Tie a pole or a piece of rope between two trees and drape your sheet over it, pegging out the sides. The ridge need not be very high and the ends can be turned in to make a groundsheet.
2. The wedge (fig. 43). With only one suitable tree available make a wedge-shaped tent as shown; a stout tree will give some shelter to the entrance. A piece of rope pegged out from the tree to the ground can be used instead of a branch.
3. The awning (fig. 44). This gives you more of the feeling of an open bivouac but also provides considerable shelter from the wind and rain.

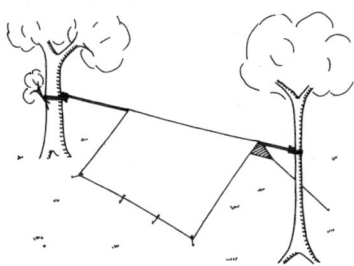

Fig. 43 Wedge tent shelter   Fig. 44 Awning   Fig. 45 Cave adapted to make a shelter

4. Combinations with natural features (fig. 45) can result in some very snug shelters. When choosing a cave to sleep in always remember that the roof and ground should slope towards the entrance for preference, or water from outside will run down into the cave.

CHAPTER NINE
Cycle Camping and Canoe Camping

So far we have only considered camping on foot, but most of what has been said is equally applicable to cycle camping and canoe camping. When on a bicycle you can see more of the country than on foot but not, of course, in so much detail, although you can always stop and explore on foot anything which particularly interests you. When travelling by canoe you enter a different world; large stretches of river and canal bank are well away from roads and often densely overgrown, so that you can easily imagine you are an explorer paddling down an unknown river. The bank is usually an excellent place to observe birds. Herons, dippers, mallard, buzzards and even kingfishers can be approached quite closely in a silently drifting canoe.

You will, of course, need to have some experience of riding a cycle or paddling a canoe before you attempt to use either to go camping. Much has been written on cycle and canoe camping for those who specialize in these activities, but let us try to pick out the important things. The rest will come with experience.

Cycle Camping

Cycle camping can enable you to visit many interesting places and there are really very few limits to what an enterprising cyclist can achieve. Fig. 46 shows Ian Hibell, one of the world's most famous touring cyclists, crossing the Sahara desert. Ian has cycled all over the world, making such mammoth journeys as the full length of the American continent from the tip of Patagonia to the north of Alaska. That particular journey took him three years to complete! Look at how carefully his equipment is packed.

Fig. 46 Ian Hibell, cycle tourist extraordinary. Ian has completed many adventurous cycle tours in all parts of the world, including North Cape in Norway to Cape Town, South Africa. The above photograph was taken while he was crossing the Sahara desert on this journey. Notice the jerry cans and water bottles needed to carry all the necessary water to get from one well to the next and the spare tyres rolled in polythene and attached to the front forks. The panniers shown are the revolutionary nylon 'Overlander' model designed by Mr. Hibell to meet the demands of his journeys in conjunction with the makers, Carradice of Nelson, Lancs., from whom they can be obtained

He is able to get all the necessities for journeys of several thousand miles into his panniers and bags.

Ideally your camping gear should be carried in such panniers and saddlebags. The rear panniers fit on to a pannier frame which is bolted to the back stays and the brake bolt. This frame should above all be strong and rigid to hold the heavy panniers firmly in place. The saddlebag is fastened to the saddle and the seat pin, and rests on top of the pannier frame. To help to keep the weight evenly distributed most cycle tourists use a handlebar bag which attaches to the handlebars between the brakes.

This can be kept clear of the front mudguard with a simple wire support which attaches to the front brake bolt. Some handlebar bags can be quickly detached and used as shoulder bags when you are shopping and may also have a map case on top which makes map reading much quicker and easier.

Never try to go cycle camping with a rucksack on your back, as this puts the weight in entirely the wrong place and you will soon suffer from backache. In addition to this the high load can be dangerous, as it is unstable and can affect your cycling.

Packing your cycle for camping is the reverse of packing a rucksack. The aim is to keep the load low to make riding easier and safer, so heavy things go in first and light ones last. The weight should be distributed so that the balance is even side to side; it would not do, for example, to have all your heavy items in one pannier and your sleeping bag in the other. Put some of the heavier items in the handlebar bag; this will help to keep the front-to-back weight distribution even. The handlebar bag is a good place to put your camera for use during the day.

Choppers and suchlike 'fun' cycles are unsuitable for cycling camping, but any normal cycle will do provided that it is roadworthy. Tyres should have a good tread and be in a good state of repair, brakes must be well adjusted and worn brake blocks should be replaced, the chain and wheel bearings should be in good condition and well lubricated, and the wheels themselves should be 'true' i.e. not buckled. Nowadays nearly all cycles are fitted with gears, and for cycle camping it is important that you have sufficiently low gears to enable you to tackle steep hills and head winds without having to get off and walk too often. When you pedal in a low gear your feet turn faster and more easily than in a high one and it is much less tiring to pedal quickly in a low gear than to strain away at a high one. If your gears feel right when your cycle is loaded all is well, but if they feel too high a cycle shop or experienced cyclist will advise you how to lower them. Usually this is achieved by fitting a set of back cogs with more teeth or a chainring with fewer teeth, neither of which should prove to be very expensive.

Before attempting a cycle camp have a local trial ride with your cycle fully loaded. The weight makes quite a difference to the handling and it will take a little time to get used to the feel of your laden cycle. Owing to the extra weight on the back wheel the steering will be 'lighter', which means that the handlebars will turn more easily and consequently the cycle will feel more wobbly at first.

A few words about riding. Do not go touring unless you are competent, used to traffic, and familiar with the Highway Code. Remember that you are very vulnerable on a cycle and always give clear hand signals to indicate your intentions. You should also be able to mend punctures and carry out other minor adjustments. In addition to your camping equipment you will need to carry a puncture outfit, tyre levers, pump, universal cycle spanner, 'stubby' screwdriver, pliers. This is a minimum repair kit and the extra weight can be shared when touring with friends.

Until you have gained some experience curb your ambitions. A strong rider may cover 70 or more miles (112 km) a day on good roads but 15 to 25 (24–40 km) will be about the right distance for the novice. Plenty of local riding before the tour will help to get you fit and prevent saddle soreness and stiffness. Unladen you should manage 15 to 20 miles (24–32 km) in an evening when you are used to your bike, but again start off gently and gradually increase your distance. Plan your tour to keep as much as possible to country lanes. Main roads are unpleasant for cyclists, noisy and foul with car exhaust fumes. The road surface may not be so good in the lanes and you should beware of loose gravel and, when passing farms, thick mud. However the peace and freedom from traffic are worth all such minor inconveniences. Finally, take care when descending hills. Do not allow the bike to gather too much speed and get out of control. A laden cycle is quite difficult to handle, so check the speed with your brakes.

If you are a keen cyclist you will find it useful to become a member of the Cyclists' Touring Club. This old-established club is the leading body for cycle touring in this country and a modest membership fee will secure access to a wealth of information and advice on all aspects of cycle touring. The club has district associations in all parts of the country which hold regular weekend meets, and there is also a well-produced magazine to keep you informed of club events and up to date on equipment developments etc. For information on the club write to: The Secretary, The Cyclists' Touring Club, 69 Meadrow, Godalming, Surrey.

Canoe Camping

The canoe is a very versatile craft and has been used from early times for penetrating wild country, particularly jungle, where the rivers are often the only clear highways. It can progress in very shallow water where other, larger craft cannot go and will travel easily in only 6 inches (150 mm) of water. Because it is light it can be portaged (carried) around obstacles such

Cycle Camping and Canoe Camping

as rapids and waterfalls. It is relatively cheap, requires little maintenance, takes up a minimum of storage space and can be transported on a car roof. With a canoe one is able to explore many fascinating waterways which are inaccessible to other craft.

Fig. 47 *Eskimo hunter in his kayak, East Greenland*

First let us clarify the term 'canoe'. Strictly speaking, a boat in which you sit, which has a deck and is propelled by a double-bladed paddle is called a kayak and was originally designed by eskimos for hunting seals in the Arctic Sea (fig. 47). In Britain we call this a canoe. The true canoe, as

Fig. 48 Canadian canoe

used by North American Indians, is paddled from a kneeling position using a single-bladed paddle and is usually undecked. This we call a Canadian canoe (fig. 48).

Either canoe or kayak may be used for flat water touring, but on rough rivers and the sea the kayak has the advantage of being difficult to swamp, owing to its deck and the fact that the cockpit can also be sealed with a spraydeck, a waterproof cover which fits over the cockpit and around the waist of the paddler. In this country kayaks are much more popular for canoeing in general than Canadian canoes and there is a great variety from which to choose. Fibreglass is now the preferred construction material; it is light, strong, and easily maintained and repaired. If you are considering the purchase of a canoe you should choose a fibreglass one. A touring canoe should travel easily in a straight line and should therefore be at least 14 feet (4.3 m) long and 2 feet (600 mm) wide with a fairly flat keel. It should have sufficient buoyancy fitted to keep it afloat following a capsize but not so much that there is no room for your camping equipment. In addition you require a lifejacket and a paddle. Paddles with flat blades and tubular alloy shafts are cheap, strong and quite suitable. The length of the paddle should be such that you can just cup your hand over the upper blade at full stretch. A spraydeck is unnecessary for flat water touring.

The biggest problem which confronts the canoe camper is that of keeping the equipment dry. A capsize is not unknown, even on calm water, and some water will always find its way into the canoe even on the most uneventful journey. All equipment should be put into bags which are a) waterproof and b) the right shape to pack into your canoe. Long and fairly narrow bags are usually the best shape for most canoes. Rubberised canvas or proofed nylon outer bags can be bought from suppliers of canoeing equipment. Polythene is best not used for outer bags, since it is easily damaged as the bags are pushed into the canoe, but everything should be enclosed in polythene bags and sealed before placing in the outer bag. As an extra precaution put your sleeping bag into two polythene bags. Do not overfill the bags; there should always be some air space to act as buoyancy should the bag come adrift during a capsize. To obtain a watertight seal fasten the bags as shown in fig. 49. Fold the neck inward from both sides and then fold it again, double it over (twice if it is long enough), and tie it tightly with cord or twist a band cut from car inner tubing round it in the same way as you would an elastic band.

When packing the aim should be to keep the canoe evenly balanced. As you can get more into the stern than the bow the equipment in the bow should consist of heavier items, stove etc. Try to pack it in tightly so that it is unable to roll about when you are paddling and take the additional precaution of securing it to the canoe. Bow bags will be kept in place by your footrest and those in the stern can be secured to the seat with nylon cord. Make sure that the bags do not dig into your back or impede your feet. A laden canoe is very heavy and you will need help to carry it to and from the water.

You do not need to be a very experienced canoeist to go canoe camping provided that you use canals and slow-flowing rivers. Whitewater (rough) rivers and the sea are for experts only. However, a few basic common-sense rules need to be borne in mind:

1. You should not canoe unless you are capable of swimming at least 50 yards/metres in light clothing.

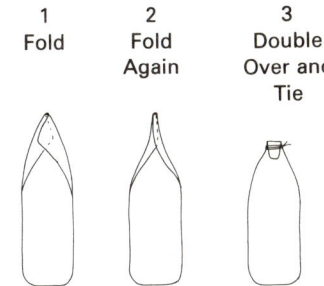

Fig. 49 Making a waterproof fastening on a canoe bag

2. You should wear a lifejacket at all times even if you are a good swimmer.

3. Never canoe alone.

4. Learn to handle your canoe properly before you go touring. As a minimum you should:

Be able to get in and out easily.

Be able to paddle forwards and backwards in a straight line without difficulty.

Be able to turn using sweep strokes.

Know what to do if you capsize *and have practised* getting out of an upturned canoe following a capsize. It is not sufficient to know it in theory.

Know how to empty your canoe if it is waterlogged.

5. Do not attempt to shoot weirs, carry round them. The water above a weir is usually calm and very slow-flowing and there should be no danger of your being accidentally swept over if you can handle your canoe properly.

6. You will meet locks on canals. These consist of a series of sluice gates which control the flow of water from one level of a canal to a lower level. Large boats have to go through the locks to change levels, but a canoe can usually be carried around with less difficulty.

Membership of the British Canoe Union is an advantage. Touring information and advice can be obtained, as can information on any branch of the sport. The B.C.U. has a very good coaching system; there are various tests which you can take to assess your ability at various levels of proficiency and there will be coaches in your area who run training courses.

Ideally you should at least be at the level of the B.C.U. Elementary Certificate to go touring. The address of the secretary of the B.C.U. is: Flexel House, 45–47 High Street, Addlestone, Weybridge, Surrey KT15 1JV.

Access to rivers is not always readily available. Before embarking upon a tour you ought to discover whether you need permission to canoe your chosen river and where you can gain access to launch and disembark. The B.C.U. river advisory service will help you with problems of this kind. You need a licence, obtainable from the Inland Waterways Board, to canoe on canals and some rivers. The B.C.U. *Guide to the Waterways of the British Isles* provides full information on all the major rivers and canals in the country, and gives an overall description of each waterway and a mile-by-mile description of features, hazards etc. along the route.

If you can plan your campsites and obtain permission before you make the actual tour, this is preferable to looking for your campsite each afternoon, which may involve several long trips over fields to seek permission before finding a farmer willing to let you camp. When using pre-arranged sites make sure that you know where they are! The bank often looks quite different from the river, so try to pick out some distinctive landmark a little way upstream of the campsite. Carry your canoe well up the bank when you stop for the night. Even though the weather may be fine where you are, heavy rain in the headwaters of the river can cause sudden flooding and some rivers may rise several feet in a few hours.

A final word, be kind to anglers! Remember that they too are entitled to an undisturbed day's sport and that in some cases they may have paid a lot of money to fish that particular stretch of water. Careless canoeing can

disturb the fish and spoil the fishing for hours. If it is possible canoe past as quietly as possible on the far side of the river if the fisherman is fishing his near bank. If he is spinning or fly fishing, however, he may be fishing the far bank and would prefer you to pass close to him. When in doubt or where passage is difficult stop well above, walk along and ask him where to pass. In some cases he might ask you to carry round. Respect his wishes; relationships between canoeists and anglers are not always of the best, and politeness, courtesy and respect for other people's needs and views can only help to improve the situation.

Good camping equipment is by no means cheap. Tents in particular are an expensive item which can easily be ruined by careless treatment. Simple maintenance and care in storage will repay itself a hundredfold in terms of the extra life which you will get from your equipment and in the knowledge that your kit is always ready for use, is in good condition and will not let you down at an awkward moment.

CHAPTER TEN

Looking after Your Camping Equipment

Tents

It is most important to ensure that your tent is absolutely dry and aired before storing it away. NEVER, NEVER pack your tent away if it is the slightest bit damp. Any dampness, no matter how slight, can cause mildew, which will rot the canvas, and the tent will be ruined. Nylon tents are not subject to attack by mildew in the same way as cotton but should still be thoroughly dry before storing. It is a mistake to assume that the tent is absolutely dry if it has been struck on a warm, dry day. Although the canvas in the main will be dry the seams around the base, where it is in contact with the ground, can be quite damp. If the weather is warm and sunny when the tent is struck, turn it over and spread it out for any moisture on the groundsheet and base to dry out before packing it away. Whatever the weather is like when you strike camp, always hang the tent out to dry and air as soon as you get home. Never leave a wet or damp tent packed in its bag any longer than is necessary.

While the tent is drying wash the mud off the pegs and then dry them. Straighten any bent pegs by gently hammering them on a hard surface or squeezing them in a vice. If any are broken or lost replace them as soon as possible. It is quite a good idea to write on the tent bag in waterproof felt pen the number of pegs and pole sections which you should have. This will make it easier to check when you have not used the tent for some time. Check all the guy lines to make sure that none are frayed, knotted or broken, and replace as necessary. Before putting the tent away make any necessary repairs to the canvas. The places which most often require attention are those which are subjected to a lot of stress; door fastenings have a tendency to pull away, corner seams and other points where guy lines are attached can start to come apart. The time to note these first signs of wear and tear is when the tent is empty and about to be struck. Make a careful inspection of the canvas, note any repairs which need to be done and carry them out as soon as possible.

Store your tent in a warm, dry place, folded rather than left rolled in its bag, as this can cause the material to rot at the folds if tightly packed.

Stoves

Stoves which are properly lit and well looked after seldom go wrong. However, it pays to carry a few spares to deal with the commoner emergencies. For both paraffin and gas stoves you should carry spare washers for the base of the burner assembly, prickers to clear the jet if it becomes blocked and a spare jet nipple and nipple key. If you have a paraffin stove you will require two more spare washers, one for the pump and one for the priming cup assembly. Trangia-type methylated spirit stoves are the ultimate in simplicity; there is nothing to go wrong and no parts to replace except the sealing ring in the lid, which is a non-essential item.

Looking After Your Camping Equipment

The following remarks apply to paraffin pressure stoves which, being the most complex, tend to have a greater number of possible faults and usually require attention more frequently than gas stoves. Fig. 50 shows a sectional diagram of a paraffin stove.

If the pump does not work efficiently it can usually be cured quite easily by unscrewing the cap which retains the pump shaft and removing the washer assembly. Grease the washer with butter or lard if at camp and ordinary grease is not available, spread it a little to make it a better fit in the pump body and replace. Should the washer be damaged or torn replace it with a new one. Note that the stove will work without the pump in place, which means that if you have more than one stove of the same kind in the party you can share a pump if one is faulty and spares not available.

With repeated pricking over a number of years the jet may become too large to function efficiently or, occasionally, a pricker may break off in the hole and the jet will have to be replaced. To do this you require a nipple key, which is a small spanner with a universal joint at the end. Insert this through the top of the burner, (fig. 51), locate it over the nipple and turn it anti-clockwise to remove the nipple. The new nipple is fitted the same way, but it is a fiddly job and you must be careful not to damage the burner thread by cross-threading the nipple.

Fumes emerging from the junction of the tank and the burner indicate that the lead sealing washer at the base of the burner is damaged or too compressed to do its job efficiently. Pick it out with a penknife or a nail and replace it with a new one.

Occasionally fumes may be seen escaping at the priming cup. If the leakage is considerable these fumes may ignite. To cure this take the

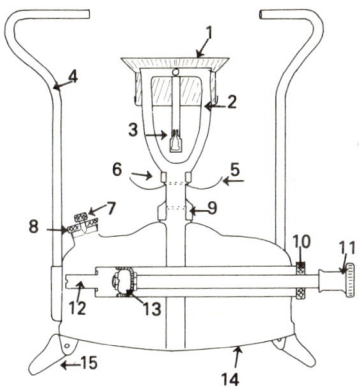

1 Flame spreader
2 Burner tube
3 Jet
4 Leg
5 Priming cup
6 Fibre washer
7 Valve
8 Filler cap
9 Lead washer
10 Pump retaining nut
11 Pump
12 Pump valve
13 Leather washer
14 Tank
15 Foot

Fig. 50 Section through a one-pint paraffin stove

Looking After Your Camping Equipment

burner apart by using two spanners, one on the nut below and one on the nut above the priming cup. Replace the washer on the priming cup with a new one and re-assemble the burner, making sure that the joint is really tight.

None of these repairs is difficult to do, but if you do not feel confident about carrying them out yourself any camping shop will do them for you.

Dixies

Your dixies should last almost a lifetime with care. Pitting of the aluminium is the biggest enemy. This can be reduced by not adding salt when cooking until the water is boiling so that the salt is quickly dissolved. Keep your dixies clean and when you get home give them a really good cleaning both inside and out. Make sure that no dirt or food is left to decay under the rim or in a corner. As a further precaution against pitting, rinse very thoroughly to remove all traces of detergent and dry very carefully before storing.

Sleeping Bags

The sheet inner should be washed after each outing but the outer sleeping bag will not require cleaning for some time. When it does need cleaning it can usually be washed at home if it is filled with one of the man-made fibres; just follow the maker's instructions. Dry cleaning is usually necessary for down sleeping bags although products such as 'Soppy', designed for home cleaning of down bags, can be obtained and are quite effective.

Fig. 51 Nipple key in use

After dry cleaning it is most important that the sleeping bag is hung outside to air for several hours. Never sleep in a bag just back from the cleaners without doing this, for the fumes from the cleaning fluid are extremely toxic and several people have died through ignorance of this fact.

While at camp be careful not to damage the bag. Nylon outers are easily damaged by contact with hot objects such as the stove legs. Any hole caused by a burn or a tear should be patched immediately. This is particularly important with down sleeping bags, as the precious filling will soon be lost and also you will emerge from your bag looking as though you have spent the night in a hen-house! As an emergency measure stick a plaster from your first aid kit over the hole until you get home.

Store your sleeping bag loosely folded in a warm, dry place. Do not leave it tightly rolled in its container, as this will compress the filling, whether artificial or natural.

Insurance

Once you have assembled a good set of camping gear it is advisable to insure it against loss or damage. Prices are rising all the time and a stolen rucksack full of camping equipment could be a very expensive item to replace. Premiums are quite reasonable, usually about £1 per annum for each £100 worth of equipment insured and you can include your watch, camera and other sporting equipment.

If you have not used your camping equipment for some time, always check to see that it is all complete and in satisfactory condition before you leave for camp, even though you know that you checked it thoroughly before putting it away. It is a bit late to do anything about it when you arrive at camp to find that mice have eaten a big hole in your sleeping bag or that you have not got your tent poles because your mother moved them to a different place and forgot to tell you about it! It is surprising just what can be wrong with supposedly sound equipment and a quick check may save you a lot of hardship.

CHAPTER ELEVEN
Camping Checklists and the Country Code

When packing for a camp it is quite easy to forget some small but essential item. Imagine getting to a campsite well out into the wilds and finding that you have no matches to light the stove. It has happened to many people. Errors of this kind are easily avoided if you keep a list of the things which you need to take and check each item off as it is placed in your rucksack. As you become experienced you will develop your own preferences for certain items of equipment, but in the meantime here are my camping lists, to which you can add any other items you would like to include.

General
- Tent
- Flysheet
- Stove
- Dixies
- Spare fuel
- Water container
- Toaster
- Knife, fork, spoon
- Mug
- Plate
- Panscrub
- Foam mat
- Candles and holder
- Matches
- First Aid equipment
- Map
- Compass
- Whistle
- Torch
- Boot polish and brush

Personal
- Sleeping bag
- Sheet inner
- Towel and soap
- Toothbrush and paste
- Anorak
- Overtrousers
- Spare shirt
- Spare vest
- Spare pants
- Spare socks
- Spare sweater
- Handkerchief
- Gym shoes
- Woollen hat
- Book
- Cards
- Diary
- Pen
- Camera
- Money

Below is the Country Code, a set of simple but important rules for all who go into the countryside. Remember that the country is home and a place of work for many people who will appreciate your presence much more if you always observe the Country Code and respect their way of life.

Good camping!

The Country Code

1. Guard against all risk of fire

A carelessly discarded match or cigarette could destroy large areas of woodland which have taken many years to grow and all the wild life which lives within them.

2. Fasten all gates

Sheep and cattle will soon stray on to roads or into fields of growing crops if gates are left open, causing the farmer considerable work and expense.

3. Keep dogs under proper control

An untrained dog can cause a lot of harm by chasing livestock. Remember that your dog can be shot if caught worrying sheep.

4. Keep to the paths across farm land

Growing crops are easily spoiled by people walking across them and some crops may look just like long grass. Resist the temptation to take a short cut across a field; if there is no obvious path keep to the edge.

5. Avoid damaging fences, hedges and walls

If you keep to the footpaths you will always find gates or stiles. Fences, hedges and drystone walls are easily damaged by people attempting to climb over and are very costly to repair.

6. Leave no litter

Litter is unsightly, and also bottles, cans and polythene bags are dangerous to livestock. Help to keep the countryside beautiful by taking all your refuse home. Better still, why not always try to take home a little extra?

7. Safeguard water supplies

Do not put anything into or near water which may pollute it. Be particularly careful about toilet arrangements when camping.

8. Protect wildlife, wild plants and trees

Wildlife in Britain and many other parts of the world is under great pressure from the numbers of people visiting the once wild areas. Try not to disturb wildlife but learn to observe it. If you see a beautiful flower, photograph it or make a sketch. Do not pick it; there may only be a few like it in the country or even the whole world.

9. Go carefully on country roads

This really applies to adults who drive cars. Country roads are often narrow and winding and there may be dangers around any corner, such as a flock of sheep or a tractor. Even on your bicycle it pays to take care.

10. Respect the life of the countryside

Try to understand and visualize the problems which visitors can cause for farmers and others who live and work in the country. If you know the problems there is less chance of your unwittingly offending a country dweller by your behaviour.

Some More Books to Read

Canoeing Complete by Brian Skilling. (Kaye & Ward 1973)
Camping and Hill Trekking by Squadron Leader P. F. Williams. (Pelham 1969)
Camping and Woodcraft by Horace Kephart. (Collier-Macmillan 1947)
Guinness Guide to Bicycling by J. Durry. (Guinness Superlatives 1977)
Guide to the Waterways of the British Isles. (British Canoe Union)
The Hike Book by Jack Cox. (Lutterworth 1965)
Modern Canoeing by Charles Sutherland. (Faber 1964)
Nature is Your Guide by Harold Gatty. (Collins 1960)
A Thousand Miles in the Rob Roy Canoe by J. McGregor. (1881 & Canoeing Pub.1963)
Richard's Bicycle Book by R. Ballantine. (Pan 1975)
The Worst Journey in the World by Apsley Cherry-Garrard. (Penguin 1979; first published in 1937)

Index

'A' pole (of tent), 20, 21
Awning shelter, 64

Backpacking, 14
Bacteria, 50
Bell end, tent, 22
Bicycle, 66–70
Billies, 40
Bivouac, 61
— sheet, 64
Boulder flap, tent, 23
Brakes, bicycle, 68
British Canoe Union, 74
Bulldog pegs, tent, 24
Buoyancy, canoe, 72
Burner, primus stove, 39

Canal locks, 74
Canadian canoe, 72
Candle holder, improvised, 41
Candles, 41, 51
Canoe, 66, 71–6
Canoe camping, 70–6
Carriage candles, 41
Chain, bicycle, 68
Chainring, bicycle, 69
Checklists, 83

Closed cell foam, 37
Cooking, 52–6
Corner guys, tent, 24
Country Code, 84
Cycle camping, 66–70
Cyclists' Touring Club, 70

Dixies, 40, 46, 80
Dried foods, 53
'D' rings, tent, 24
Dry cleaning, 80

Egg cups, 54
Entrances, tent, 22

Fibreglass, 72
Fire risk, 40
Flooding, 57
Flysheet, 19, 20, 21, 29, 32, 57
— extended, 22

Gas stove, 37, 38, 46, 78
Gears, bicycle, 68
Grommet, tent, 20
Groundsheet, 18, 32, 50, 62
Guy lines, tent, 23, 27, 28, 78

Handlebar bag, bicycle, 67
Hibell, Ian, 66
Howff, 13
Hygiene, 59–60

Inland Waterways Board, 75
Insulation, 36, 37, 63

Jet, paraffin stove, 79

Karrimat, 37
Kayak, 71–2

Lifejacket, 72, 74
Lighting, tent, 40, 41
Lightweight camping, 13–15

Main guys, tent, 24, 32
Matches, 51
Methylated spirit stove, 37, 38, 78
Mildew, 77
Mobile camping, 14
Mountain tent, 22

Nipple (jet), paraffin stove, 79
Nipple key, 79
Nylon tent, 77

Index

Packing, 45–7, 68
Packframe, 43
Paddles, canoe, 72
Pans, 40
Pannier frame, bicycle, 67
Panniers, bicycle, 67
Paraffin, 46
Paraffin stove, 38, 78–9
Petrol stove, 38
Pitching (tent), 26–32
Poles (tent), 20–1
Polythene, 62, 64, 73
Polythene bags, 45, 51, 57, 59
Prickers, stove, 51
Priming fuel, 39
Primus stove, 38, 45
Proofing, tent, 18, 19, 25
Pump, stove, 79
Pyramid tent, 21

Repair kit, bicycle, 69
Ridge pole, tent, 21
Ridge tent, 18, 21

Rucksack, 43, 63, 68
— frame, 43
— packing, 45

Saddlebag, bicycle, 67
Separator, tent, 21, 29
Shelter, 48–9
Shelters, 63–5
Side guys, tent, 24, 32
Side walls, tent, 23
Skewer pegs, tent, 24, 32
Sleeping bag, 35, 45, 80
— sheet, 36
Sleeve entrance, tent, 23
Slider, tent, 24, 27
Snow valence, tent, 23
'Soppy', 80
Spraydeck, canoe, 72
Standing camp, 13
Static camping, 14
Stoves, 37–9, 78–80
Striking (tent), 32–4
Surface tension, 19
Survival bag, 61
Synthetic fibres, 35

Tent pegs, 23
Tents,
— arranging, 51–60
— choosing, 16–25
— pitching and striking, 26–34
Toaster, 53
Torch, 40
Trangia stove, 38, 78
Tyres, bicycle, 68

Unit tents, 19–20

Waste disposal, 59–60
Water container, 42–3
Waterproofing, see Proofing
Water supply, 50
Wedge tent, 22
Wedge shelter, 64
Wheel bearings, bicycle, 68
Wheels, bicycle, 68
Wood fires, 39